Ego Niches

Other books by Harold J. Morowitz

Ego Niches

An Ecological View of Organizational Behavior

by
Harold J. Morowitz
Professor, Yale University

Illustrations by
Sidney Harris

OX BOW PRESS
Woodbridge, Connecticut
1977

Second Printing

Library of Congress Catalog Card Number: 76-48568
ISBN: 0-918024-01-3

Printed in the United States of America

TO MATTHEW AND HIS GENERATION

Preface

It may seem presumptuous for one who is not a professional psychologist or sociologist to offer a book on organizational behavior. Nevertheless, I have spent many years working in organizations and observing the actions of those around me. As a biologist I have constantly sought an explanation of the ofttimes perplexing behavior of my co-workers. Using the insights of evolutionary theory, ecology and the newly emerged science of ethology, it has been possible to develop a theoretical framework within which to understand many of the puzzles posed by the activities of individuals working within the system. That theory is the subject matter of the following pages.

This book owes more than I can express to the efforts of three people. My friend and mentor in the English language, Ozzie Bushnell has patiently counseled me and has aided in removing infelicities from my prose. His blue pencil traces out a path of wisdom. My wife and editor Lucille has constantly urged me to call a spade a shovel. Her blue pencil traces out a path of love. My son Noah has proven to be an apt observer of ego niches. He has provided numerous perceptive examples from his academic experiences. His blue pencil traces out a path of youthful iconoclasm.

H.J.M.
Woodbridge, Conn.

Contents

Ego Niches

Chapter 1

Organizations and Ecological Systems

This work has been entitled "Ego Niches" to emphasize the fact that insights from ecology and social psychology have been combined in order to obtain a new and deeper concept of the behavior of individuals functioning within organizations. There has been a trend in recent years to study the interactions of animals in nature as a prelude to gaining a better understanding of the behavior of man in society. In the following pages let us explore this application of Natural History to the most uniquely human of inventions—institutions and organizations.

After taking note of C.P. Snow's concept of the two cultures, we cannot expect that those thinkers who are concerned with organizational behavior will possess a thorough knowledge of the natural sciences. Therefore, because our analysis is so rooted in biology, it will be helpful to review some of the principles of ecology that must serve as a background. Those readers who may be averse to the language of science are asked to be patient; the relevance of these findings to humanists will emerge speedily. No doubt as a tribute to Lord Snow's insight, the overuse of technical jargon in social writings has been referred to as "a snow job." It is a practice we shall not indulge in.

An ecological system is an association of different kinds of organisms and the surroundings in which they live together. The word "ecology" is derived from a Greek term meaning a house or, as we would say now, a habitat. Examples of such systems are a pond, a forest, a coral reef, or a desert, together with all the creatures, great or small, plant or animal, that dwell in those places. The animals and plants that live in any one system are of many different kinds, and each kind of creature is a member of a group that is called a species. The problem of defining a species with precision is so difficult that many biologists now regard such attempts as specious. Interestingly, even Charles Darwin, author of *Origin of Species*, confessed to having trouble in defining the concept of a species, and biologists have tended to ape Darwin ever since. In any event, the difficulty will now be avoided by declaring that all the members of a given species are similar in form and function, and furthermore, that all members of a single species perform approximately the same role within a given ecological system.

In any ecosystem, then, each species is either a producer or a consumer. Producers take energy from the environment and convert it into forms that are useful to themselves and eventually to other organisms. In most natural ecosystems, the *primary producers* are the algae and the higher plants that carry out photosynthesis, which is a process by which the radiant energy of sunlight is converted into the chemical energy stored up in molecules of sugar and starch that, in time, other organisms can use as foods. In these chemical changes achieved by photosynthesis, carbon dioxide and water are used up and oxygen is produced.

The *consumers* in natural ecosystems are the animals, who gain their sustenance either from eating plants or from eating other animals that have eaten plants. Ultimately, all of the organisms living within an ecological system are able to function because the primary producers, the photosynthetic plants, have converted solar energy into chemical energy.

Now the first analogy can be drawn between mankind's organizations and nature's ecological systems: *the operation of both kinds of systems is totally dependent upon primary productivity.*

Let us examine the functions of organizations in order to clarify this statement. Generally, the primary productivity of an organization is the avowed reason for the existence of that establishment. Thus, the principal activity of a trucking firm is in moving freight from one place to another, and the firm's primary producers are its drivers and freight handlers. The main purpose of a mining company is in the extraction of an ore from the earth, and its producers are the miners. The most essential function of an educational system lies in transmitting information (and occasionally wisdom) from teachers to students, and the classroom participants are the primary producers. A police department has as its avowed goal the maintenance of law and order in a community, always, of course, within the limits imposed by the constitutional guarantees of freedom. Here the basic producers are the patrolmen and detectives.

Examples of ecological systems can be extended indefinitely, and from all of them two important generalizations emerge:
1. The primary producers are those individuals who are placed at the bottom of the organizational chart.
2. All members of the organization other than primary producers exist because of the activities of the primary producers.

An interesting extension to the first generalization can be drawn: in our American society, at least, the primary producers are the first group of employees within an organization to be unionized. We shall return to this observation after we have had a chance to discuss further the relationships between producers and consumers.

The fact that organizational productivity is the result of the work done by people in the lowest levels has long been recognized by economists. In assessing the ratio of output to input in any system, the inputs may occur at any organizational level, but almost invariably the output is most directly the work of the lowest level—the primary producers.

One of the most serious difficulties that modern institutions encounter comes from the failure of people installed in the intermediate levels of the organizational chart to recognize the second principle we have presented above, namely, the inescapable fact that employees at all higher levels depend for their very existence upon primary productivity.

This problem will be elaborated upon in a later chapter. At the moment we must be content with illustrating by example the origin of the difficulty. Consider a scientific research organization, whose primary productivity is the performance and evaluation of experiments. The primary producers are the laboratory scientists, the technicians, the dishwashers, and other such related personnel. Above this primary level in the organizational chart will be the hirelings in management, fiscal administration, report writing, personnel, purchasing, and the like.

Now it may happen, for example, that a fiscal officer forgets (or confuses) the principle of primary productivity, and assumes that the main purpose of the organization is to produce budgets and fiscal reports. He will conclude, then, that the main reason why the research operation exists is to provide something about which budgets are to be prepared and fiscal reports are to be written. If the organization yields to this inverted and perverted concept of ecology, the finance office grows at the expense of the research operation, thus increasing the costs for overhead that must be supported by genuine primary productivity. An unchecked population explosion of this sort ultimately leads to ecological catastrophe—an organization that is all overhead with no primary production. Obviously, such a situation is unstable, and leads to a total collapse. Many organizational breakdowns result from this type of failure because someone who should have known better has forgotten what constitutes primary productivity. An especially dominant personality entrenched at an intermediate level is very likely to commit this kind of error in assessing the organization's function. Such an individual is a threat to the structure and success of the entire operation. The theory of ego niches will explain such behavior, and thereby will also suggest the remedy for the problem.

Returning now to nature's ecological systems, let us examine what happens to the products of photosynthesis. First, they are used to maintain the life processes of the photosynthesizers themselves. Second, they are consumed by another group of organisms, called herbivores or grazers, who may eat the fruit, the root, the sap, the leaf, or the entire plant. Thus another ecological level of organisms consists of those animals that directly derive their energy from eating whole plants or only parts of them. The survival of organisms at this second level is absolutely dependent upon the existence of the first level. The disappearance of the primary producers would cause the herbivores to starve to death.

7

A useful jargon has evolved among ecologists, in which the primary producers are designated as "the first trophic level," while the herbivores and grazers are called "the second trophic level." Generally, in human organizations the positions analogous to that of the second trophic level are filled by people who interact directly with the primary producers. Thus foremen or forewomen, time keepers, guards, delivery boys and delivery girls, some secretaries, and others whose function derives directly, and at only one step removed, from the efforts of primary producers can be considered as members of the second trophic level.

Ecologists also recognize a third trophic level, which consists of carnivores, or organisms that derive their energy directly from eating herbivores. Of course there are cases of organisms that are both herbivores and carnivores, which eat fruits and vegetables as they are found, and at the same time act as predators upon certain kinds of animals grazing in the ecosystem.

In human organization the analog of the third trophic level includes both middle management and record-keeping operations that go beyond the tallying by which the second level keeps track of the first. As in biological instances, the stratification into trophic levels is not rigid, and an individual in middle management may interact directly with both primary producers and occupants of the second level. In most organizations the chain of command does not strictly correspond to functional levels, so that the working system actually forms a network rather than a ladder. In ecology a strict ladder would be a "food chain," but in fact natural systems consist of "food networks."

Last but not least are the top carnivores, or members of the fourth trophic level, those animals that get their food by preying on other carnivores. In general, an ecosystem can support relatively few top carnivores, because there are so many diversions and losses of usable energy all along the lower levels in the food network. Thus a large amount of primary production is necessary in order to support a population of herbivores. The conversion from primary productivity to that at the second level is only moderately efficient. About ten pounds of grass are needed to make one pound of cow. Needless to say, a given herbivore population can support only a limited number of carnivores, and further reductions in ratio appear in the number of top carnivores that can be sustained by carnivores.

In organizations, top management plays a role analogous to that of top carnivore in natural systems. In a very real sense top management is predatory upon middle management and is limited in its growth and range of activities by the amount of money flowing through the organization in consequence of primary activity at the first level. Thus, top management (like top predators) are the least important part of the system—with respect to the *production* of energy. We shall later see, however, that they do play a role in keeping the successful system in proper balance. The close analogy between organizations and ecological systems arises from the fact that they are both hierarchical and pyramidal in nature.

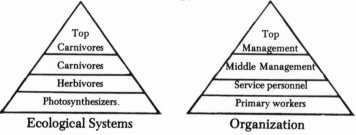

Ecological Systems   Organization

In this context, the word "hierarchy" means a body of persons or things ranked in grades, one above another, from lowest to highest. This term, which enters our considerations through biological usage, comes from a Greek word meaning "high priest" and thus has its origins in one of the oldest of human organizations. Indeed, John Milton applied the concept of hierarchy to angels and archangels, thereby extending our organizational theorem upwards by another—and extra-mundane—rank.

Both natural ecological systems and human organizations are composed of organisms operating at different levels of function, in which the members of one stratum feed upon those in the layer immediately below. In other words, the activity of each level derives from the productivity of the next lower one. Only a single level is productive in the real sense, and all the others derive their existence from that activity.

We hasten to assert that our analysis should not be taken as an endorsement of the first trophic level only, and a condemnation of all higher tiers, either in natural systems or in people's organizations. That way lies catastrophe. Nature, after all, is determinedly neutral in matters of ethics, and all organisms in an ecological system have their destined roles to play. If there were no herbivores, the unrestrained productivity at the first trophic level would soon clog the system. Indeed, there are some dry forests where very few herbivores dwell, and periodic fires must take the place of grazing animals in thinning the system of its excessive plant population. A mininum number of grazers are necessary in order to keep the ecosystem from becoming entirely static. Thus, completely egalitarian utopian theories, such as the one advocating "the dictatorship of the proletariat" fail to recognize the paramount ecological fact that a system consisting of only one trophic level is inherently unstable and therefore impossible. The function of management in both communist and capitalist societies is to keep order in the system by insuring that primary productivity is directed, arranged, and limited.

The agents who impose control must be supported by the net productivity of the "workers," and this requirement leads inevitably to the establishing of trophic levels in one form or another. In this lies the aptness of the comparison between human organizations and nature's ecosystems.

Consider an example of overgrowth among members of the first trophic level at the expense of higher strata. When a clear lake is polluted with mineral nutrients as a result of human activity, such as introduction of sewage, the algae of the first trophic level "bloom" and outgrow all the herbivores around them until they literally clog up the lake with their bodies, thereby killing off many members of the higher levels in the process. The lake is converted into a smelly, slimy, clogged-up mess. In ecologists' terms, it has become eutrophic, "well-fed." Eutrophication is a common problem nowadays, and the classic example of an ecosystem in such terrible disarray is Lake Erie.

An organizational analog to this perilous condition, involving overgrowth at the first trophic level, occurs when the primary producers, through overzealous union activity, acquire such a large share of the gross productivity that an insufficient amount remains to support the rest of the system. An example of this occurred in the New York City newspaper industry during the 1950's and 60's. An aggressive group of unions representing workers of the first trophic levels, such as

11

printers, typesetters, and pressmen, vigorously pursued a set of goals, and through a series of strikes were able to win for themselves a very large share of the income. Not enough of the paper's resources was left to support members in the upper trophic layers, and an instability developed. That soon led to organizational collapse, and a number of newpapers went out of business. Thus, the New York *Mirror*, the New York *Journal-American*, the New York *Sun*, the New York *World-Telegram*, the New York *Herald-Tribune*, and Lake Erie stand as examples of untimely death due to eutrophication.

We can examine also the case of a system that allows overgrowth of the herbivores. The fate of a number of Pacific islands serves as an example of this phenomenon. Before the advent of Europeans, these islands were in relatively good ecological balance. The plants were eaten by insects, lizards, and birds, which were in turn eaten by insects, lizards, birds, and people, all of this leading to a reasonably stable situation. Captains Cook, Vancouver, and others of their helpful kind upset the natural ecology by introducing cattle and other large grazing animals to the islands. Soon the domesticated livestock escaped to the forest, to roam as wild creatures. Before long there was a population explosion among these animals of the second trophic level, leading to hordes of cattle chewing up the plants of the first trophic level, overgrazing the islands, and converting what were once lush tropical paradises into relatively barren wastelands. Some sensible balance could not be restored until the introduction of "artificial carnivores," gun-toting men who were given the specific job of preying upon the population of wild goats, pigs, sheep, and cows.

An organizational equivalent to overgrazing can be found in

"THIS IS TERRIBLE. IF THE PLANKTON GO OUT ON STRIKE, IT'LL DISRUPT THE ENTIRE FOOD CHAIN."

almost any public welfare system. In such a system, strange as it may seem, the primary producers are the disadvantaged poor, the recipients of the organization's concern. Their welfare is the avowed purpose of the organization, and within it each hierarchical level is founded upon the primary activity of the welfare recipients in using up the money alloted them. The fact that users are primary producers may sound odd, but really, the welfare situation is no different from that of schools, where teachers and students are the primary producers. Cash may percolate from top to bottom in such organizations, but functional productivity flows from bottom to top.

The second trophic level in a public aid organization consists of the social workers who dispense funds to the recipients. In such an organization the number of case workers may undergo a population explosion. More and more of the available funds are diverted to paying the case workers' salaries and, naturally, less money remains to be spent for welfare. As a very direct result people must be removed from the welfare rolls—and in theory the number of poor decreases. What happens in bitter fact is that the case workers of the second trophic level are "overgrazing" the provender of the first trophic level, the money intended for poor people. To say the least, this is an unstable situation that eventually will lead to collapse of the welfare system, or to revolution, or to some other kind of violent but necessary readjustment within the system.

If the carnivores of the third trophic level are not limited by top carnivores, a special kind of process known as oscillation occurs. Ecologists sometimes refer to this as the "cabbages-rabbits-foxes problem." We illustrate it by an imaginary habitat that is occupied by only these three species. Assume that cabbages are growing well and that enough rabbits are present to keep cabbages from overgrowing the place. The rabbit population in turn is kept in check by the foxes. The foxes are unchecked, however, and soon they achieve a population explosion. Now the overpopulation of foxes eats up rabbits faster than even rabbits can reproduce. The result is that the fox population continues to increase and the rabbit population decreases. The greatly reduced number of rabbits leads to two consequences: first, the cabbages are undergrazed and grow without control; and second, the foxes cannot find enough rabbits to eat and die of starvation. The result is that the number of cabbages goes up as that of foxes goes down. When enough foxes die off, the remaining rabbits find a super-abundance of food and few foxes to bother them. Now the rabbits have a super population explosion, referred to as a "bunny boom" by some whimsical life scientists. Whereupon the huge number of rabbits provides abundant food for the hungry foxes. The large rabbit surplus means that foxes have plenty of food and rise in numbers, while cabbages are overgrazed and go down. However, few cabbages and many foxes means that the rabbit population must decline and the entire cycle begins again. The oscillations may continue indefinitely, although inexorably, or they may grow in magnitude until the system collapses. This type of behavior in organizations of humans has not been studied as yet, but suspicions are growing that some of the cyclic variations in the stock market are due to the activities of uncontrolled carnivores, so to speak. Clearly, it is merely accidental that bears are classified among the Carnivora, while bulls are herbivorous. Pigs, to complete the listing, are omnivorous.

15

Owing to the inefficiencies of conversion along the way, it is extremely unlikely that a serious overgrowth of top carnivores would ever take place in a natural ecosystem. However, analysis of organizational behavior among human beings may point out the instability of such a situation. Consider the American railroad industry as an organization whose main purpose is to transport people and freight from one place to another. After the initial growth of the railroads, during the last century, control over them shifted to the so-called "robber barons," one of the most predatory groups that has existed in American business life. The robber barons occupied the fourth trophic level in the American economy and attempted to manage the system so as to make almost all of the productivity flow into that high level. They made no allowance for either the growth or the maintenance of the lower levels. In consequence, the system collapsed from its own weight, and only governmental aid and subsidies prevented a complete debacle. In retrospect, the explanation is obvious: the top carnivores subverted the organization's basic purpose from transporting people and goods about the country to transporting money from the pockets of stockholders and railroad users into the pockets of robber barons. The avowed purpose and the actual purpose were at odds, and the barons' machinations led to imbalance, collapse, and readjustment. Pigs, bulls, bears, foxes, rabbits, and cabbages: all sloshed around for a while in the mire, until a new set of balances was attained. Thus does life go on.

Without further moralizing, we suggest that the instances presented in this chapter might well be pondered by members of all trophic levels in all organizations. Unchecked tendencies toward imbalance always lead to disastrous instabilities—

unless some mid-level carnivore is smart enough to head them off before they come to pass.

Chapter 2

The Basic Theory

The correspondences between organizations of men and ecological systems in nature that we have been discussing leads us to examine the work of biological scientists in an effort to better understand the institutions people have created and the functions they expect these artificial assemblages to perform. This examination has given us some clues for comprehending the behavior of individuals in structured hierarchies which is encompassed in our theory of Ego Niches. But, before we proceed much further, let us define what we mean by this concept of niches.

The notion of an ecological niche is highly specific, and here the word "niche" is used in a sense quite different from that of its everyday meaning. The dictionary's third definition comes closest to the scientist's intention: "a place or position adapted to the character or suited to the merits of a person or thing." The ecological niche occupied by a species in a living system is a consequence of its adaption. It is, in effect, the role that the species plays in a natural system by virtue of its function, its behavior, and its relation to other members of the system. In an organization the equivalent of this definition of a niche would be a job description. Thus, Eugene Odum writes in his textbook *Ecology*, "Ecologists use the term habitat to mean the place where an organism lives and the term *ecological niche* to mean the role that the organism plays in the ecosystem; the habitat is the 'address' so to speak, as the niche is the 'profession.' Thus we can say that the kangaroo, bison, and cow, although not closely related taxonomically, occupy the same niche when present in grassland ecosystems."

The usefulness of the niche concept is that it relates what a species does to the structure and function of the whole ecological system. To extend our analogy, a niche definition is a job description superimposed upon an organizational chart, and so written as to relate that job to the functional activities represented by the chart. The niche has been a useful concept in dealing with ecological systems precisely because, to coin a phrase, "no species is an island unto itself," and because the study of species in terms of niche behavior stresses those relationships that are most important in understanding functional ecology. Often within a given habitat there is intense competition among species attempting to occupy the same niche. Within a given species, furthermore, there may be intense competition among individuals for a limiting resource. Some of these problems have been perceived by the wise Dr. Seuss, and we can do no better than to quote his pronouncement:

And NUH is the letter I use to spell Nutches
Who live in small caves, known as Nitches for hutches.
These Nutches have troubles the biggest of which is
The fact there are many more Nutches than Nitches.
Each Nutch in a Nitch knows that some other Nutch
Would like to move into his Nitch very much.
So each Nutch in a Nitch has got to watch that small Nitch
Or Nutches who haven't got Nitches will snitch.

The comparison between organizations of human and ecological systems makes it clear that the notion of a functional niche is a perfectly straightforward concept to use in describing and studying organizations. However, there is one outstanding difference between ecological behavior and organizational behavior. *Each individual in an organization has an ego role to maintain that is independent of the functional role for which he was hired.* This inexorable compulsion of the ego to play its role is a characteristic of every single human being, and is derived from his sense of individual self.

As a result of this aspect of human behavior, each individual plays a dual role in an organization: a functional role determined by the job description for his position in the overall activity of the organization; and an ego role determined by his own demanding psychological needs. The ego role leads him to make for himself an ego niche in the structure of the organization which may be quite independent of the normal activities of the institution and, indeed, often may be in conflict with them. This awareness of the dual role of an individual in an organization is the main hypothesis in the theory of Ego Niches.

The postulate may be restated from another perspective: *Each individual in an organization engages in two distinct types of activities, one related to the nominal purpose of the organization and the second related to the demands of his own ego.* A second postulate, less firmly documented although universally recognized, states that: *In general, the higher the trophic level occupied by an individual in an organization, the greater is the amount of time he devotes to ego functions as compared with organizational functions.* The reason for this will become clear later, if it is not sensed already. Many of the problems of inefficiency and deterioration encountered by organizations are the direct result of arrangements which allow people who are preoccupied with ego roles to subvert the functional roles they should be fulfilling.

Thus we have stated the first two laws of the theory of Ego Niches. If they seem obvious, it is but a tribute to their validity; for obviously, a truth once stated has been in the backs of all our minds. If the postulates seem simple, all profound laws of science are simple—once they are stated. Thus the laws of thermodynamics can be written in two lines, although a lifetime is required to understand all their consequences.

At this point it might be well for us to offer a few blatant examples of acts which are designed solely for establishing or defending ego niches and therefore are counterproductive in terms of organizational function.

*A middle-management executive calls in his secretary and says, "Would you pick up that scrap of paper from the floor and put it in the waste basket." It is apparent to everyone that no function of value to the organization has been served by this deed; in fact, such interruptions seriously impair the working efficiencies of such a martinet's secretaries, not to mention their morale (which is but a familiar way of saying their egos). The act is explainable only in terms of the egregious executive ego expanded to a point almost beyond deflation.

*Research groups within a university have a simple procedure by which, in an emergency, purchase order numbers can be obtained and requisitions can be made by telephone for items that are needed in a hurry. Suppose the director of the purchasing section issues a three-page memo stating that henceforth such purchase numbers will no longer be issued over the telephone, but that instead the requisitioner will have to appear in person at the purchasing office to fill out a series of forms. The university's research groups are scattered through a dozen or more buildings in a large city, some of them almost a mile away from the purchasing office. Moreover, needless to say, no parking space is ever available near the purchasing office. At the very least the director of purchasing is being counterproductive in terms of the function of the organization. In soberest fact, he is elevating his own ego and its role merely to gratify it at the cost of harmony in the organization. He is no longer the efficient chief order clerk which he should always endeavor to be; instead he imagines himself a policy maker, a person to be reckoned with.

*A top-level executive orders a new and gorgeous carpet for his office floor, to replace an attractive and functional (although perhaps more modest) covering installed by a recent predecessor. This act of conspicuous consumption, so costly to the institution, is simply an announcement telling everybody about whose ego is important now in the organization.

The remaining chapters of this scholarly inquiry into vagaries of humankind will offer a descriptive study of the kinds of ego niches that exist in modern organizations and the kinds of people who occupy them. We will simply detail our experimental results without going into methodology, lest the author seems to be seeking sympathy for the arduous days, weeks, and months he has spent in field work in factories, mines, offices, schools, government agencies, churches, and homes while gathering the wealth of data from which these samples are chosen.

A critical inspection of our extensive case histories reveals a second fascinating correspondence between the behavior of creatures examined in nature and that of people met in organizations: *the strategies that are used to acquire and defend ego niches by members of the human species can be matched by rather exact counterparts in ecological behavior strategies that are used to maintain species within their niches in natural habitats.* A comparison of human ego niches with examples from the sciences of ethology and ecology throws considerable light upon the mechanisms concerned with ego defenses. It is almost as if, in human beings, Jungian archetypes from our evolutionary past were evoked from the collective unconscious to equip us with a vast number of botanical and zoological strategies nature has made available for the work of protecting our egos.

But, before we can proceed with our appraisal of the survival kits handed down to us by our own natural heritage, we must spell out in more detail what is meant by the word *ego*. The term as we use it here is employed in an everyday sense, just as the people who spoke Latin intended it, avoiding as much as possible the complex accretions and rather elaborate assumptions that have followed Freud's dissection of the psyche. The ego, for our purposes, is the self, or the sense of self, that each of us possesses. For most of us the ego is rather a private notion, or perhaps an opinion, because—as philosophers have stressed for a long time—we can never quite know what's going on in another person's mind (if indeed we can ever be sure about what's happening in our own!). Yet, in another sense the ego has a public aspect, since the sense of self is not an abstract and isolated relationship but derives from our interactions with other people and other objects. More often these definitions of ego are not stated explicitly; but, nonetheless, vague as they are, they impel us along through life as we wander about in our search for ego-gratifications.

In modern society the ego as we have described it is an extremely unstable entity. It continually feels threatened by competition and change, and just as constantly it needs support and reassurance. In an organization of egos, the individual's ego needs to feel that the person it possesses is playing a significant role, regardless of what is actually happening in real life. Individuals yearn for the security of knowing that their existence in the organization is justified. After all, if one's presence is not essential to the success of the institution one is always threatened with the possibility of being cast out from the haven of that organization. Thus ego security is linked with job security—and often goes much deeper.

In addition to ego problems imposed upon him by his place within the organization, each individual brings to his job all those hang-ups which he has spent many years in acquiring. The wounds of a lifetime of psychic inputs, going all the way back to the time of bed-wetting, deprivation of breast feeding, and a nightmarish horde of other traumas, accompany each of us wherever he goes. The inescapable slings and arrows of outrageous fortune suffered in experiences outside his organization leave their marks upon an individual and sensitize him to the need of defending his ego within the institution in which he earns a livelihood.

People working at the primary production step acquire relatively fewer ego problems from the organization, although externally-generated ego problems may appear at any trophic level. In general, primary level functions are so practical that a worker finds little reason to question the necessity of his function in the system. As one climbs the organizational ladder, however, ego justification becomes more and more necessary. Accordingly, the higher up in the hierarchy one gets, the farther one moves from primary productivity and the greater is the tendency to divert more effort into ego functions. In the automobile industry, for example, if one works on the production line welding together the parts of a chassis, few occasions arise for one to question the importance of that activity. On the other hand if one sits in the customer complaint department sending out form letters to disgruntled buyers or if one is in charge of giving psychological tests to employees—ah, then one so easily feels that insatiable gnawing at the ego, telling him that the company could make its cars perfectly well without relying on that particular function—or without one's precise self! In much the same way as conscience is defined as "that wee small voice that tells you when you are about to be caught," so the hypersensitive ego may be imagined as constantly hearing wee small voices suggesting to a guy or a gal that all is not right in the world around.

The phenomenon of what happens to an ego as it rises through the levels of a hierarchy was illustrated on television a few years back by the situation comedy "Arnie." The hero, Arnie, was elevated suddenly from being shipping-room foreman to vice-president in charge of developing products. Many of the show's episodes dealt with ego problems encountered within the executive echelons of the company. The story of Arnie started by showing him, content and efficient, as a member of the company employed at the second trophic level, with a small degree of overlap into the first trophic level. He had few ego problems beyond those relating to his interactions with the group of workers he was supervising. Then, suddenly, he was made a vice-president.

He became a top carnivore and after that much of his activity on the job went into his own ego-swelling functions and those of the rest of the top carnivores. Somehow the show was funny. It showed the comic side of the ego niche crisis that we shall be examining in a more serious vein.

The correlation between the importance of ego roles and the advance of individuals within the hierarchy makes contact between our theory and the Peter Principle. Dr. Laurence J. Peter, founder of the science of hierarchiology, declared that *"In a Hierarchy Every Employee Tends to Rise to His Level of Incompetence"* and proved his postulate with many uncomfortable illustrations. As one consequence of this principle, the higher you look in a hierarchy, the more likely you are to find a position occupied by someone who is incompetent for that job. In addition, our own analysis based upon innumerable examples gained from every kind of institution shows that the higher up the ladder a person moves, the less likely will his job be related to primary productivity. When these two principles are consolidated we arrive at the awesome conclusion that the higher one looks in a hierarchy, the more likely one is to find incompetent people doing unnecessary work totally unrelated to the primary purpose of the organization. One pauses to wonder: do those vast exercises in ego-posturing and ego-niche defending arise at the top levels of an organization because the executives have little else to do? Or, is ego vaunting one of the necessary prerequisities to executive achievement?

In the past the structural charts of most organizations were highly pyramidal: the number of individuals decreased sharply at each trophic level. Since the industrial revolution has come along, the primary producers have been the aggregate of people *and* of the machines they use, and therefore the number of people engaged at that level decreased. Since the computer revolution, a number of second level tasks are being performed by machines. As a result a greater percentage of the employees of many organizations are moving up into higher levels of management. The new pattern of distribution serves to exacerbate the problems arising from ego functions and leads to a significant increase in numbers and kinds of problems within the organization.

The classical pyramidal structure of organization does explain, however, why unionization almost invariably occurred first at the lowest level, that of primary producers. Because that level involved large numbers of people, the relative role of a single person compared with the sum of all the workers at that level was minimal. Moreover, large numbers of primary producers are interchangeable in their jobs. Thus the individual workers were the most vulnerable people in the structure, in spite of the absolute dependence of the system upon their collective output. The response to this real threat to individual security was unionization. The phrase "real threat" is used here to contrast it with threats to the ego. When they establish unions, people are responding to forces that menace their livelihoods, their economic security. On such occasions, when bellies are gripped by hunger, egos are forgotten—at least for a while.

With these general considerations borne in mind, we proceed to demonstrate our theory by describing actual ego niches. We shall do this by considering animals or plants in field observation taken from nature, and then by indicating the equivalent behavior among human beings drawn together in organizations. We shall compare the ways in which certain people defend their egos in an organization with the methods used by certain lower organisms to defend their ecological niches in nature. If some of these comparisons prove to be uncanny in the closeness of fit, we must remember that the grass and he who mows or smokes it are descended from a common source. The walrus, the carpenter, and the oysters all have a common genetic heritage stretching back into the early history of our planet. Perhaps the matter has been put best by that great braggard Pooh-Bah, who reminded us: "You will understand this when I tell you that I can trace my ancestry back to a protoplasmal primordial atomic globule."

Chapter 3

The Octopus Niche

Although most of us have had very little direct contact with an octopus, some behavioral patterns in organizations of people are so suggestive of that strange underwater creature that the correspondence is eerie. It is as if we humans still carried in our chromosomes certain genes that are shared with these denizens of the deep by virtue of inheritance from a still more primordial ancestor of both species. On the other hand, the phenomenon may be less mystical than we imagine. Both the octopus and its organizational counterpart have persisted until the present by cruel use of all those devices of cell and brain and muscle that ensure the survival of the fittest. A strategy which works for one creature in one stress situation may prove to be effective for another creature in an analogous situation. Biologists have long talked of "convergence," the similarity of distantly related forms which occupy similar habitats and niches. Thus, the placental anteater, and the marsupial anteater, although only distantly related, have evolved to achieve a similar size, shape, and method of feeding as a result of the similar functions they perform. Perhaps we would approach nearer to the rational spirit of our time if we regarded the similarities between the benthic octopus, deep in the sea, and his human counterpart, inhabiting the land, as displays of the amazing power of convergence under varying environmental stresses. Cultural evolution no less than biological evolution is capable of eliciting strange forms.

In nature, the octopus is a shy, bottom-dwelling animal that spends most of its time hiding among rocks or in crevices on the floor of the ocean. Indeed, this propensity for crawling into small holes has done in many an octopus: people living along the coasts of the Mediterranean soon discovered that tying a narrow-mouthed earthenware pot to a rope and then dropping it to the ocean floor was an effective means of catching an octopus. After a few hours, the submerged pot was hauled up to the surface and frequently contained an eight-legged delicacy to grace the fisherman's table. On occasion the octopus has to leave the safety of its home to search for food, thereby exposing itself to large fish, sharks, and other predators. When threatened by one of these carnivores, the octopus responds in a unique manner: he squirts out a large mass of black ink that so beclouds the water around him that the pursuer is unable to see the fleeing creature swimming or crawling off to the nearest refuge. Some octopuses are said to release a cloud of ink which so resembles an octopus that the pursuer goes after the imitation rather than after its true objective.

The octopus niche in organizations is likely to be occupied by a technical expert in the middle echelons of management. This kind of specialist normally lurks in a small office, surrounded by technical books and desk calculators. Every available bit of space is filled with file cabinets, creating a habitat not unlike the submarine grotto among the rocks where his zoological counterpart lives. Ordinarily, this insidious individual is not much noticed, although in fact a few tentacles of his may be reaching out, prying into other people's business.

When threatened by a predator—that is to say, by someone

31

in the top levels of management—the organizational octopus responds with an enormous outpouring of ink, thereby making the situation so murky that his ego can crawl back unnoticed into the office-grotto, there to be secure among the familiar appurtenances. Here the term ink is used in its classical sense. But in his feat of obscuration, the modern octopus supplements the direct use of real ink with memoranda, computer printouts, Xerox copies, mimeographed reports, charts, graphs, photographs, and other technologically advanced ways of distributing the communicational fluid—even on serious occasions, a real honest-to-goodness note, laboriously scrawled by hand.

As an example consider the following scenario, concerning a crisis in a certain office building in Detroit. Mr. Top Carnivore: "Mr. Cephalopod, your marketing analysis indicated that people this year would show a preference for chartreuse and vermilion cars. As a result we produced ten thousand of each kind. But at mid-year we have an inventory of 9,927 chartreuse and 9,789 vermilion automobiles. What went wrong with your analysis?"

Mr Cephalopod: "Well, as you know marketing analysis is an enormously complicated science. Rather than give you too hasty an answer at this point, I'd like a few days to compare the original report with the sales data."

That evening, just before closing time, Mr. Top Carnivore received from Mr. Cephalopod a three-page, single-spaced memo headed "Preliminary Report on the Follow-Through Study Relating the Chromatic Preference Study to Chromatic Preference as Analyzed from a Statistical Study of Sales Data." The thrust of the memo is that the study has commenced. Scattered throughout are subtle hints that the original data given to Mr. Cephalopod, upon which he based his first report, were not in the proper form, and that—even more heinous!—the advertising department had sabotaged the sale of chartreuse and vermilion cars.

The following mid-morning Mr. Top Carnivore received a large package with a note, "To keep you posted, I'm sending you a copy of the raw data we are using for the follow-up study." The package contained 19 pounds of computer printout listing the color and serial number of every car sold in the first three months of the year.

That afternoon, just before closing time, Mr. Top Carnivore received a second memo indicating the methods of the follow-up study. The memo contained very strong implications that the polling company hired to obtain responses to the company's original questionnaire about color preferences had used improper sampling techniques, and had actually selected a population skewed by three-hundredths of a standard deviation toward 12 year-olds, unmarried mothers on welfare, and motoring fanatics already owning three cars. Also noted was the fact that the pollsters did not show samples of vermilion and chartreuse but simply identified the colors by name. Attached to this memo was a copy of Mr. Cephalopod's original report, two copies of the polling agency's report, 45 Xeroxed pages from statistics books, and 23 pounds of computer printout correlating serial numbers, colors, and states where the cars were sold.

This scenario continued through nine working days and 238 pounds of material. The profusion of ink discharge rendered the waters so murky that obfuscated Mr. Top Carnivore simply ordered the unsold cars repainted a fashionable sepia. Humming tunelessly but contentedly, Mr. Cephalopod retreated to his office, to begin upon next year's report on "Chromatic Preference Among Car Buyers."

Occasionally the occupier of an octopus niche becomes so impressed with the ego protection afforded by ink squirting that he indulges in it all the time, instead of wisely reserving it for periods of stress. With little regard for the nominal purpose of the organization, he diverts all his efforts to ink squirting. When this dire stage is reached, if the organization is to survive it must either get rid of the octopus or so isolate him that he seethes in massive pools of his own ink without diffusing it upon members in the institution. Needless to say, such an obsessive squirter never runs out of ink.

The compulsive organizational octopus has forgotten the wise and moderating words of Lord Byron:

> But words are things, and a small drop of ink,
> Falling like dew upon a thought, produces
> That which makes thousands, perhaps millions, think.

Chapter 4

The Peacock Niche

Wanting to absolve ourselves of any charges of male chauvinism, we hasten to state, categorically and unambiguously, that the peacock ego niche can be occupied by either males or females. While our credentials as liberated progressives do not allow us to recognize any differences at all between males and females, nonetheless as biologists we must assert that, at least in certain species, we can discern slight differences between sexes, under some circumstances. For example, take the case of the black widow spider. The female is ten times larger than the male. The female bites, the male does not. At mating time, the female entices the male into her nest and both engage in a courting ritual that ends in copulation. After the act is consummated, the female kills and devours the male. Constitutional amendments and Common Cause not withstanding, we entertain some doubts that we should respond in exactly the same way toward a male black widow as to a female.

The peacock is the male member of the genus *Pavo*. The female is called a peahen. The male, on the average, is considerably larger than the hen and possesses long, ornately designed and colored tail feathers that can be erected and spread in an enormous fan, in a gaudy display of resplendent allure and gallinaceous sexuality. The sole purpose of this preening exhibition is to attract the peahen as a prelude to the sexual act. In contrast, the peahen is rather small and very drab, and she totally lacks the many-hued array of tail feathers. But she is a good forager and a better provider than the male. The proud beauty of the peacock makes him little more than a poseur, and a gene-donor, somewhat awkward in finding food and avoiding predators. He carries around that great weight of gorgeous impedimenta for the sole purpose of making himself attractive in the eyes of his lady bird.

Among human creatures, the organizational peacock niche usually is established near the lower end of the company hierarchy. Even so it may be encountered at all levels up to that of the top carnivores. Moreover, as we have already declared, because of the unparalleled adaptability and versatility of the human species, members of either sex can assume the role of peacock. The human peacock is concerned with attracting members of the opposite sex. Inarguably, this is a function that has very little to do with the purpose for which the establishment was founded—unless, of course the establishment happens to be an escort service or a house of prostitution. All too frequently, in the usual human organization, the holder of the peacock ego niche can be an extremely disruptive influence.

A few illustrations will make clear the nature of this niche and the effect its occupiers can achieve. Consider Miss Bird, recently employed as a file clerk in a record-keeping department. Miss Bird's ego function is entirely unrelated to filing time sheets, but is deeply involved in being attractive to the opposite sex. The only things Miss Bird files with enthusiasm are her long finger nails. After a month of not being sufficiently noticed in her new job, Miss Bird discovers the peacock niche. Her hemline begins to come up and her

"DO BE CAREFUL. WE'RE NOT SURE IF THAT'S HIS STATEMENT OR IF HE'S PARODYING PEOPLE WHO MAKE THAT KIND OF STATEMENT."

neckline begins to go down. The tint of her hair assumes a brighter hue. She is, in effect if not in fact, spreading her tail feathers to get attention. And does she ever get it! Every one of the 27 females and 19 males who work in the same section start to spend too much time watching Miss Bird. Indeed, each morning the subject of special interest to everyone is what she will be wearing—or not wearing—for the day. There is no need to detail the obvious disruption provoked by her display—or the worser consequences of the havoc she will cause among susceptible males, whether or not they qualify for the mating role.

Or take the case of Mr. Pavo, a fifty-year-old executive who has worked his way to the top and has had very little fun while doing it. Suddenly aware of the approach of his declining years, he takes a new interest in all members of the opposite sex and subtly glides into the peacock ego role. He starts his new way of life by going to the gym twice a week, determined to diminish his paunch and swell his biceps. He stops going to his plain old neighborhood barber and frequents a fancy hair stylist. Where once upon a time he sat enthroned in his office and growled at petitioners come from afar, as a good top carnivore should, now he initiates inspection tours of all offices occupied by women of any age and allure. He buys clothes with the mod cut and the European look while his neckties and shoes become more dazzling. More and more of his time, efforts, and thoughts go into satisfying the demands of the peacock role, while less and less attention are given the boresome affairs of good old Acme Wire and Tube Corp., Ltd. Alas for the females who come within reach of those wrinkling claws! Alas for the saddening fate of this vain peacock, come to his preener's roost much much too late. . .

A third case in point is Miss Ruffled Feathers, who is forty years old and the office manager. She is single, and militantly proud of it, but she is somewhat disappointed in her limited social life. And now, from her high perch, she too conceives a new image of herself and quicksteps into the peacock niche. She begins with perfumes, which—gradually but not too gradually—change in content and intensity from the tasteful, to the merely pungent, to the overwhelming, to the unabashedly menacing. Not having Miss Bird's other odds and ends of equipment, she opts against the body display but compensates for that deficiency with jewelry. Rings, pendants, necklaces, earrings multiply like cats in an alley on a moonlit night until, ere long, Miss Ruffled Feathers resembles a mobile display rack in a costume jewelry store. Bedecked with all of this sumptuous apparatus for drawing the rounded and unbelieving eyes, she tinkles, rattles, clicks, jangles, and resounds in all directions, announcing her approach to all but the deafest ears. Her final mode of display, calculated to make a mere peacock screech with envious rage, is a series of high-fashion wigs done in a wide spectrum of unnatural colors and in a veritable gallery of artificial styles.

The peacock ego niche is a common one, of course, if only because something of the peacock lies waiting in each one of us. But when this instinct for display gets out of control, and reaches a point where it becomes dangerously intrusive or distressingly ludicrous, the other fowls in the barnyard, in terror or out of mercy, must attempt to restore a balance. For the perplexed executives of Acme Wire and Tube Corp., we recommend assigning Miss Bird, Mr. Pavo and Miss Ruffled Feathers to the same small office, in accordance with the avian world's first two laws, birds of a feather flock together, and let the feathers fly where they may. In such proximity, maybe enough feathers will be shed to release the workers beneath.

Chapter 5

The Beaver Niche

The beaver is a large rodent assigned by taxonomists to the genus *Castor*. The animal is best known to us for his habit of felling trees when he wants to construct lodges and dams for himself and his family. The determination and vigor with which he pursues these endeavors has won him a high reputation among people whose trees have not been gnawed down for the beaver's sake. Some of this respect for the hard-working creature has been transferred to his counterpart among people. Whether or not we snicker when we say it, the term "eager beaver" still mixes admiration with rue.

Before turning to the human organizational beaver let us consider some of the prodigious tasks performed by his natural counterpart. *Castor canadensis*, the North American beaver, weighs between forty and sixty pounds. A husky specimen, using only his big front teeth, can fell a tree five inches in diameter within three minutes. These miniature Paul Bunyans have been known to gnaw down trees a hundred feet tall and proportionately thick. The large rodents construct their houses of branches and twigs plastered over with mud. Entrances and emergency exits for a beaver lodge are placed under water, as a means of protection from animal enemies. If the surrounding water is not deep enough, the resident beavers construct a dam, thereby altering the environment to suit their needs. These industrious animals live on a diet of tree bark and

41

aquatic plants. Before winter sets in, they establish an underwater store of food. When the water freezes, they can reach the stored foodstuffs from the lodge by swimming under the ice. If trees needed to make the dam are too distant, beavers will dig canals in order to float the logs to the place where they will be used.

The beaver is somewhat like the human animal in that he actively alters the environment to suit himself, rather than passively adapting himself to his surroundings. From the beaver's point of view, that's good, but from the ecologist's point of view, that's bad. All such egocentric animals are menaces to the environment. For the beaver, like the ruthless pioneer, in rushing to carry out his own work manages to dam things up for everybody else. Therein lies the story of the organizational beaver.

The beaver niche is occupied, in general, by an extremely insecure individual who is overanxious to please his bosses in order to preserve his position. As a result, he responds by attempting to do great quantities of work—always biting off much more than he can chew, even more than the hundred-foot trees that are attacked by his natural counterparts. The problem with the organizational beaver is predictable: just as with his rodent model, his work piles up around him until it dams up the flow of things for everyone else.

Two examples will familiarize us with the occupants of this ego niche. Consider Ms. Castor, recently hired to write copy for an advertising agency. Her employer asks her to spend the next two days writing advertisements for a new detergent which is guaranteed to cause no harm to the environment. This claim can be made in all honesty and with no intent to defraud: the detergent is quite insoluble, and doesn't rinse out of the clothes.

Ms. Castor works all day without a lunch break. She spends her evening in the library reading all about detergents and ecology. She goes home and writes for four hours. After three hours' sleep she is back at the office, composing copy for the entire day. She goes home, naps for a couple of hours, and writes through the night. The following morning she deposits on her boss's desk 47 versions of the ad, all lauding the new product, so that he can choose the one he likes best. Her boss got his executive job in the agency by being a graduate of Yale-with "a gentleman's C," of course. His lips would get tired if he had to read the copy for 47 different ads. He calls four of his colleagues to his side and they begin reading. Unfortunately for those young geniuses, all of Ms. Castor's ads are so good that choosing among them involves an incredible amount of discussing, arguing, and deciding. All other executive work is jammed to a halt. Four days later the number of alternatives has been reduced from 47 to 34. Clearly, this little beaver has dammed up the habitat for everyone else.

Mr. Flattail, a recent graduate in management from the University of Oregon, is given a junior executive position in the personnel section of a large company. He wants to succeed. In fact he is so eager to succeed that he leaps instantly into the beaver ego niche. His formal job is simply to screen applicants for office positions and then to send them along to several managers to interview. He reasons that the more applicants for a position the better for the company, so he begins by seeking them. He starts with the State Unemployment Office and the local business colleges. He scans the "Positions Wanted" ads in the newspapers from communities for fifty miles around. He tries the local high schools and inquires after their recent graduates. Not wanting to indulge in discrimination, he sends friendly letters of brotherly concern to the NAACP, the Black Panthers, the Young Lords, to the B'nai B'rith, Hare Krishna and the Moslem Brotherhood, and follows these with discreet inquiries addressed to representative groups of Japanese American, Chinese Americans, Chicanos, and American Indians.

He succeeds beyond his wildest dreams. A line of applicants folded around the block appears, looking like the crowd trying to buy tickets for the opening day of the World Series. The company—fearful now of being accused of discrimination, racial, sexual, political, or religious, and terrified of the observant eye of government officials, looking for evidence of unfair labor practices—must interview every single one of the candidates. Four temporary personnel officers are hired, and all office managers are sent into the line, to devote their time to interviewing. For three weeks all normal executive functions are suspended. The beaver has done his work too well.

If you have a beaver in your organization, you have to save it (and him) by persuading him not to give so much of a damn. Alternatively, you can loudly praise him for his zeal, acclaim his diligence far and wide, and allow him to be stolen away by the competition. Then sit back and enjoy the peace and quiet of your smoothly-running organization. No institution of human beings can long endure a super eager beaver. And none of them is as patient—or perhaps as fatalistic—as is Canada. Confronted with real beavers, a natural force it could not get rid of, Canada elevated the creature into a model to be respected, and put his portrait on the first postage stamp it ever issued.

Oddly enough, the most famous eager beaver of all time did not develop in a capitalist country but lived in the Soviet Union. Aleksey Grigoriyevich Stakhanov, all by himself, mined 102 tons of coal in a single work shift. Working in the 1930's he consistently exceeded production norms and set new ones. In 1935 the state began a propaganda campaign urging all workers to imitate Stakhanov, who could hardly have been popular with his fellow miners. Soviet children joined societies of Young Stakhanovites. It has been reported that the higher production norms led to excessive pressure on other workers and throughout the Soviet Union quality of goods was sacrificed to quantity. For a time the eager beaver niche for everyone was the goal of state policy in the Soviet Union. Wiser heads finally prevailed, and one hardly ever hears of good old Aleksey any more.

Chapter 6

The Yeast Niche

So far we have dealt with niches established by animals which are relatively easy to see. Our next investigation of natural history takes us into the realm of microorganisms. Because we shall be reasoning from the unseen to the seen, a heavier burden will be placed on our imaginations as we attempt to visualize the ego role corresponding to that of yeasts. Certain kinds of yeasts, as you no doubt remember, are some of mankind's greatest helpers, making possible the rising of bread and the brewing of beer.

However, we'll not romanticize these yeasts from an anthropocentric point of view. Rather, we shall view the creatures of the genus *Saccharomyces* from a more microbial perspective— or from the far yeast, as one might say (just this once). Viewed from within the vat, the individual yeast cell is an organism that spends all of its time working single-celledly to raise the alcohol level of its surroundings to the ultimate point. When, finally, the alcohol being produced reaches a high concentration, the yeast cells that did it are sprawled out all over the place, inert and no longer able to function as proper yeast cells should do. They have worked very hard to reach the point of insensibility.

The yeast ego niche is one of the most common of all those found in the world of organizations. It is occupied by people who defend their sensitive egos by putting enough alcohol into the inner environment to reach a point of insensibility to ego-assaults, either external or internal. The yeast ego niche is frowned upon at lower hierarchical levels, tolerated at middle positions, and ignored or even encouraged at upper rungs. The reason for this trichotomy is clear: alcoholism is inconsistent with real productivity, and therefore is an absolute bar to function at the primary level. As an individual is removed from real productivity, however, the significance of spending many periods of non-productive time becomes less important to the organization, which actually continues to produce very well without him. Thus the usefulness of wall of obfuscation, as a device to protect the ego, is more and more apparent.

Consider an executive, Mr. Sy Cerevisiae. His day begins with an early flight from New York to Chicago. Before he reaches an altitude of 20,000 feet he is being offered Screwdrivers and Bloody Marys. By the time the tempting stewardess arrives at his seat with the soothing potion, the exact change she takes for her wares is burning a hole in his pocket. Soon after arriving at O'Hare Airport, just two tiny bottles of vodka later, he spends a short time in his business conference. At 11:45 he and his associates go out to lunch, which begins with two double martinis—"very dry, please." At three o'clock the meal ends, and —with 2 ounces of vodka, 4 ounces of gin, one ounce of brandy, and a whiff of vermouth gurgling around in him—he returns to the office for a brief session of planning.

Then, by arrangement, our whirling executive meets an old friend at a downtown bar, and they reminisce for 4 scotches' worth of maundering about "the good old days." Sy Cerevisiae then returns to this hotel room, hurries through the cleansing shower, and dresses to take a client out to dinner. At 7:30 they

"To Louis Pasteur, a great humanitarian — the man who kept beer from turning sour."

commence the ritual with a dry Rob Roy, followed by a second and drier Rob Roy, and proceed to a dinner served with a bottle of fine Beaujolais. Dinner ends with a brandy. The client goes dutifully home. Our homeless executive returns to his hotel where, being terribly lonely, he seeks the familiarity of the standardized bar. After consoling his lonely heart with a double bourbon and branchwater,followed by a bourbon and water nightcap he stumbles off to bed. At a minimum, the statistics are impressive: 2 ounces of vodka, 4 ounces of gin, 6 ounces of scotch, 2 ounces of vermouth, 16 ounces of wine, 3 ounces of bourbon, and 2 ounces of brandy. By assiduous applications of alcohol, our executive has rendered himself immune to threats against his ego. Also, be it not forgotten, he has managed to do about one hour and twenty minutes of real work in an eighteen hour period of company time, as his per diem expense account will show, most scrupulously.

Another example is Ms. Ethyl Naul, a middle-aged accounting supervisor who has been elevated to the position from that of bookkeeper, both too soon and too late. She has reached her level of incompetence—and she and all her underlings soon become aware of that fact. Ethyl's ego comes under constant attack in this exposed elevation, and she lunges after ego protection.

The yeast niche suggested itself to her, most insidiously, when one day she noticed that the afternoon passed much more bearably after she'd had a cocktail at lunch. Soon she discovered that a before dinner cocktail made the evening much more acceptable. If a little medicine is a good thing, she asked herself in the manner of all such forlorn folk, then why not increase the dose? Quick as a shot, Ms. Naul's evenings came bottled in bond. She became a total yeast by night, wholly immersed in her comforter, and she barely functioned by day. Because she had always been incompetent at her supervisory job, her inability to work was scarcely noticed by any one. The yeast niche provided her with a medium for survival. Until one evening when, stepping into the bathtub with a bottle of warming gin in hand, she knocked her head on the tub's hard edge, dropped the bottle into the bath, slid smoothly into the welcoming maelstrom, and attained the rewarding insensibility of the compleat yeast by drowning in the brew she herself had made.

"Done in by Gin,"
Her headstone should have read
But on it, with charity, they put instead
"Fallen, only to Rise again."

The essence of the yeast ego niche, we note the moral, lies in the use of chemical reagents to fuddle both mind and psyche to a point where ego problems are lost sight of in a nimbus of azure haze. Reagents other than ethanol are being used currently but the niche is the same—salvation by obfuscation.

Curiously, this ego niche has a classic poet laureate in Omar Khayyam.

"Drink! for you know not whence you came, nor why,
Drink! for you know not why you go, nor where."

"The Grape that can with Logic absolute
The Two-and-Seventy jarring Sects confute:"

"Oh Thou who didst with pitfall and with gin
Beset the Road I was to wander in."

Little more need be said of this niche. Each of us knows it all too well.

Chapter 7

The Howler Monkey Niche

Sometimes, within an organization, a group of people will join forces to create an ego niche that can be managed only as a shared experience. This kind of cooperation corresponds to behavioral systems exhibited by some social animals which defend their territory by means of group endeavor. One such ploy met in human organizations corresponds rather closely with that used by certain Central American primates and is designated herewith as the Howler Monkey Ego Niche.

In the jungle areas lying between North and South America live several species of large monkeys belonging to the genus *Alouatta*. The distinguishing feature of this group of primates is the development of a large resonating cavity directly off the windpipe, which permits these animals to produce a loud, cacophonous noise—that is to say, a howl—whenever they wish to do so.

The social habits of howler monkeys center about the pack or the extended family, a group of about thirty animals which travel together through the portion of the jungle that is their home territory. There is only one pack in each such domain, and each pack jealously guards its homeland. On occasion two packs meet at a territorial border. Thereupon a symbolic battle immediately takes place, in which every member of each group howls at the others as loudly and as vigorously as he can. This chorus of noises is accompanied by belligerent

51

posturing. After a while one or both groups will retreat from the border—and the shouting match is over, as silence settles once again over the jungle. Other threats to the pack that might appear at the border are treated in much the same manner.

The important feature of this type of behavior lies in the fact that the territory is "owned" by a group rather than by an individual, or by a mating pair, as is often the case among birds or fish. The defense of the threatened ground is the responsibility of the entire pack.

Since egos among human beings tend to be highly individualistic, cooperative ego niches among them rarely exist. However, the phenomenon *is* known—and when it occurs defense of the niche most closely resembles the howler monkeys' defense of their threatened territory.

The point can best be illustrated by another of our poignant examples. Let us imagine a parts department at a manufacturing plant that is run by a supervisor and six stock clerks. Their territory has natural borders, since they are located at the far end of a building and are separated from the rest of their universe by a waist-high counter which effectively walls them off from the community Out There. No one who is not a member of the elite pack is allowed to pass the counter and enter the sacred precincts. The territory is so crossed by ceiling high shelves and enormous bins that numerous protected recesses exist. Within these cozy spaces, members of the pack spend most of their time talking and partaking of coffee and doughnuts. Spending the major part of the day at chattering and eating is, of course, typical primate behavior. A single sentinel usually stands guard at the border of the territory, poised to warn of impending danger. When, in our hypothetical manufactory, the territory of the parts department is approached by apparent threats, such as a top carnivore or more than two primary producers, the sentinel begins the tactics of defense:

"Hey Joe," he shouts, "shelve the number 17 widgits!"

From deep within the jungle of shelves and bins a second howl arises: "Hey, Pete! Bring the fork lift."

A third member rushes up to the front, screaming, "What's the order number of them 74 pipe frazzles?"

From the rear comes a loud voice, clearly that of an overburdened, overworked man: "Hey, I'll need some help out here on the loading platform."

Another member of the pack staggers to the counter and deposits a huge carton of paper towels. He groans wearily. "Damn it, they should pack these in fifties instead of in hundreds."

Other voices chime in:

"Hey, where are the number 87 point 543 bolts?"

"Come on you guys, I need help on the platform."

"Check the shelves back there for an 892 female wenchit."

The shouting goes back and forth until the whole territory and the environs far beyond its border echo with furious roarings, while pack members rush back and forth from the inner recesses to the jeopardized frontiers. The noise level rises to decibedlam as the fork lift's motor grinds away and heavy cases are dumped noisily upon the floor.

By this time the threatening animals from outside can only withdraw, stunned into a state of awe by the howler monkeys' clamor.

Chapter 8

The Pufferfish Niche

In the tropical waters of our planet lives a strange and fascinating family of fish known to scientists by their family name Tetraodontidae. This group includes the globefish, the pufferfish and the porcupine fish. Perhaps the best known member is the *fugu*, a pufferfish which is a culinary delicacy among certain Japanese gourmets. It makes an exciting meal for those daring enough to try it. Although the flesh is delicious, the gonads and some of the digestive organs, especially the liver, contain a deadly toxin which must be removed most carefully by a trained expert in order to make the flesh safe to eat. But among the many surprises that life can offer is the opportunity for even the best qualified expert to make a mistake now and then. The taste thrill experienced by the eater of *fugu* may be followed, very soon, by a stronger effect that sends the diner most precipitously on a trip to meet his ancestors. Often, he is accompanied on this hurried departure to the next world by the fugitive spirit of the expert who, out of chagrin at this insuperable proof of his ineptitude, kills himself.

Our interest in these plectognaths is not directly concerned with the toxicity of their gonads and other viscera, fascinating as that might be, but with a strange behavioral adaptation that these fish have evolved. When a predator approaches them, they respond by taking air or water into a special sac connected with the gullet, and immediately puff up to several times their normal size. The pursuer, upon seeing how his expected tasty morsel has been converted into something large, ominous, and ugly, becomes discouraged and shies off, looking for other fry to fish for. Some species of plectognaths have added other deterrents to their armamentarium: spines or barbs on the outside of their bodies that make them look like huge pin cushions when they have puffed themselves up.

Once again the organizational counterpart to our model from natural history is recognizable. Which one among us nice, decent, agreeable, hard-working guys and gals has not tangled with the petty bureaucrat who guards his ego (and his niche) by puffing himself up out of all proportion to the dimensions of the job he is supposed to fill? Indeed, the essence of petty bureaucracies lies in a series of puffer fish ego niches, each characterized by a ritualistic display designed to enhance the puffer effect. The puffer is not often found in an office at the very top of a hierarchy, because the primary fact about the niche reserves it for creatures who, in the deflated state, are really quite small. Nonetheless, when a person too small for his job is installed in a position at the upper level, and he realizes that he is terribly insecure in that high office, he can very easily metamorphose from a spineless minnow into a prickly puffer.

Sometimes one encounters a whole sequence of puffers in series. I am reminded of a trip I made to a museum once, with the hope of using its film library before the official opening hour at 10 A.M. Upon trying to enter the hushed sanctum, I was accosted by a tall stout man garbed in a uniform suitable only for a Field Marshal in the Kingly and Kaiserly Army of Bosnia and Herzegovina. On his chest, above the medals, orders, and decorations, he wore a plastic badge which proclaimed him to be " M. Tetraoda—Portal Officer." Now let me assert right here and now, that, in my opinion, being a doorman is an honorable profession. But for an organization to call such an honorable man a "Portal Officer" confers upon him, at once and by definition, the worst features of a puffer.

M. Tetraoda demanded of me my ID card. I produced a University identification card and meekly stated the purpose behind my unwonted visit. Alas, neither ID nor bearing offered sufficient proof of civic virtue and spotless rectitude. I was directed to a nearby window labelled, "Senior Portal Officer." Behind the window, in his grotto, sat R. Jones, equally gorgeously uniformed, very busily shuffling through a stack of papers, supremely unnoticing of my presence. A fit of piteous coughing by my temerarious self finally aroused Mr. Jones from his taxing labors and I repeated my petitioner's request. Mr. Jones, after the obligatory rumination, consented to say that he would arrange an appointment for me with Ms. Fish in the Division of Temporary Identification Certification. M. Tetratoda was summoned, very grandly, to escort me, very ceremoniously, to Ms. Fish's office—where I was instantly put down as a presumptuous upstart by Ms. Fish's secretary (who must have been from the pit viper ego niche, judging by the way she recoiled and hissed at me).

After waiting for 10 minutes, I was ushered in to see Ms. Fish, a businesslike yet pompous young lady, who very soberly addressed a number of extremely important questions to me, such as what is the country of my birth? and what is the highest academic degree I hold? Finally persuaded (if not convinced), she issued an elaborate set of identification papers as well as a temporary identification badge embedded in plastic. At last, just as the doors were being opened to admit the general public, I was released to go about my scholarly business. Eternally impressed with the commanding importance of Generals M. Tetraoda and R. Jones, and of guardian goddess Ms. Fish, I tiptoed away, desperate to find the men's room.

The puffer niche may take many forms. One of the less formidable of these is the dropping of Big Names, or the casual mentioning of academic degrees and prestigious alma maters. Another of the puffer ploys most frequently practiced is inaccessibility. One of the distinguishing characteristics of a certain type of puffer is that he can be found behind his closed office door, doing nothing, even while his secretary out front is explaining why he is too busy to see anyone. With him, helpful fellow that he is, you can always make an appointment to see him in two weeks. All too frequently, however, the puffer's secretary will telephone you later to change the time of the appointment because the puffer has been called away suddenly, to attend a vital meeting.

If you have a legitimate reason for discussing the organization's business with someone and he is too busy too often to see you, you may assume one of two conclusions. Either he is a poor administrator, who has not learned to delegate authority, or he is a puffer who is protecting his ego by striving to convince you how important he is.

The administrative hierarchy in public school systems seems to have more than its fair share of officials in the puffer niche. There is, for prime instance, the assistant principal who is too important to spend his time talking to mere teachers, or the principal who is too busy to talk with students. And the district superintendent who waves his doctorate around for all to see and is much too big a man ever to find time for meeting with parents who wish to speak to him.

The puffer is very costly in terms of an organization's function. Although frequently he busies himself conspicuously, he is not doing his proper job because he is too busy showing that he is too important to be doing his job. A habitual puffer begins to take himself so seriously that all too often he convinces others. A characteristic of puffers is a conspicuous lack of humor and a total lack of insight into the use of the self-inflation process as a device for protecting the ego.

Chapter 9

The Pigeon Niche

The American bard of humorous poetry, Ogden Nash, once wrote "There is nothing in any religion, that forces us to love the pigeon." Regardless of Nash's theology, we can hardly disagree with his sentiments, especially after we consider the pigeon ego niche.

Pigeons are members of the dove family which have adapted to sharing cities and other inhabited areas with humans. Of course pigeons must be loved by other pigeons; otherwise it would be difficult to understand why there are so many of them. The pigeon appears to have evolved in the direction of becoming an instrument for ingesting all kinds of foodstuffs, converting them into thin whitish feces, and then dropping the products of digestion over as wide an area as possible, especially on statues. Thus a pigeon's habitat becomes covered with layer upon layer of excrement in varying stages of consistency, odor, and decay. These dive bombers of defecation leave no object untouched, as they flutter above saints and sinners alike.

Because of our unavoidable acquaintance with the excremental activities of all members of the species *Columbia livia*, we need to make only a small leap of the imagination to visualize the activities of the human types who occupy the pigeon ego niche. The organizational pigeon guards his own ego by besmirching and besmearing everyone else with all manner of crap. This kind of pigeon is always hovering around, waiting to dump a load upon anyone who comes into range. By making everyone else look bad, he elevates himself in his own esteem, if not in that of his associates. Our scenario will illustrate the foul phenomenon.

Mr. J. Columbus Bird is a junior executive in a small corporation. His office is next to that of Mr. Tom Neophyte, who works for a different section in Bird's division. They meet one morning and engage in this generous conversation:

Mr. Bird: "Good morning, Tom,—Have you noticed that the cleaning service doesn't seem to be doing as good a job as they used to. They're supposed to mop the office floors every other night, and these floors sure don't look like they did it."

Mr. Neophyte: "Yeah. They do look a bit dirty."

Mr. Bird: "Say, have you seen the new secretary Frank hired?—I've never seen such poor taste in clothes. Migawd! She looks like she gets her clothes at a rummage sale."

Mr. Neophyte: "Oh?—No, I hadn't noticed."

Mr. Bird: "Speaking of Frank, have you noticed what long lunch hours he's been taking lately? Between the two of us, I think he's having an alcohol problem. I was talking to one of the salesmen who had lunch with him two weeks ago. Whoosh!—Two double martinis tossed off before the menu even appeared."

Mr. Neophyte: "Gee, that's too bad.—By the way, when is Roger coming back to work?"

Mr. Bird: "He got out of the hospital Tuesday. They say he had surgery for hemorrhoids. But I really think he has something else—You know what I mean?"

Mr. Neophyte: "Not really.—But, say, I have to go now. Top Carnivore is going to come by soon, to check last month's operations."

Mr. Bird: "Yeah, I understand your sales were off by 14% last last month. Sorry to hear your section is having so much trouble."

Exit Tom, enter Frank Lee.

Mr. Bird: "Hi, Frank. Say, have you been having trouble with the interoffice mail service? I notice that some memos are getting held up for a few days."

Frank: "I really haven't had any problem."

Mr. Bird: "By the way, Frank, have you noticed anything strange about Tom lately? I've heard a rumor that he's having marital problems. His section had a bad month last month, and I wonder if his personal problems are affecting his work."

And so he goes, on and on, dishing the dirt, while no one dares to tell him to stop it. The organizational pigeon may work directly, or by hints and innuendoes, but his intent is always the same—to discredit everyone else in the organization. Even after many layers of thin white detritus have been spread over all the people in the entire hierarchy, the pigeon sits on his lofty trapeze, clean and pure—and undeterred. The *Columbia livia* ego is elevated by the sure knowledge of all the shortcomings of everyone else in the organization. From all of which, thanks be to the grace of the Great Pigeon God, he alone is spared. . .

Chapter 10

The Lion Niche

An institution need not be as large as the United States Army, as wealthy as IBM, or as complex as the University of Chicago in order to qualify as an organization. Indeed, one of the oldest human organizations is the family and it is within this context that we shall discuss the lion ego niche.

Lions are among the largest members of the cat family and live together in social units known as prides. A pride consists of a small number of families each composed of a lion and lioness pair and their young offspring. Two features characterize lion society: the roaring which goes on in the morning and evening and the very efficient hunting of antelopes, zebras, and other grazing animals. Zoologists are in some disagreement as to whether the lion should be called *Leo leo* or *Pantera leo*, but these academic disputes need not concern us at this time.

Among the big cats there is one feature unique to the lion which we must blushingly refer to as sexual dimorphism. Indeed, our *Encyclopedia Britannica* reminds us, macropedially speaking, of "the male African Lion, which is the only terrestrial member of the Carnivora that shows obvious sexual dimorphism." We have alluded delicately to sexual dimorphism in our discussion of the peacock and the peahen, but now we must put aside all residual prudery and face the issue. The deplorable fact of the matter is that lions and lionesses do have very different appearances. The males are larger and have a well developed mane of long hair on the back and chest. In addition, the behavior of lions differs very much from that of lionesses. We mentioned the two chief features of lion society, roaring and hunting. Well, to end the suspense, the males do all the roaring and the females do all the hunting. After the prey is captured, the lioness drags its carcass back to the lair, where the daddy lion, a true king of beasts, is the first to fill himself with the tastiest cutlets. During the day noble lions sleep, of course, while lionesses take care of their cubs.

Now we come to the ego niche in the family that corresponds to the leonine behavior we have been discussing. The niche is occupied by a male who believes that there is a biologically ordained, or divinely ordained, sexual dimorphism in humans which decrees that the male should do all the roaring around the house while the female should do all the work around the house. This niche protects his ego from the realization that he is less competent than his mate. The scenario, though familiar, is worth a brief reexamination to awaken us to the full impact of this behavioral pattern. Let us transport our thoughts to a quiet suburban house on a Sunday morning.

Felicia is whispering: "Children, please go outside and play quietly. You know your father wants to sleep this morning." A tranquil hour passes, during which Felicia dusts the furniture and sweeps the porch. Suddenly a roar emerges from the master bedroom. "Felicia, bring me the paper!—And can't you keep those kids quiet? You know I need my rest. I gotta play eighteen holes this afternoon."

Felicia fetches the newspaper, goes outside with cookies for the kids, once again urging them to play quietly. A silent thirty minutes pass while Felicia prepares lunch. Then another roar comes from the master's den. "Felicia, where in hell is my bathrobe? Why do you always hide it from me?—I can never find the damn thing."

Felicia hurries to the bedroom, takes down the bathrobe from its hook in the closet, hands it to Leon, and plods off to make him some fresh coffee. A few minutes later he appears, still roaring. "Damn it, Felicia, this kitchen table is a mess! Why is all this garbage out here? And can't you keep the kids quiet on Sunday morning?"

We will spare the readers the psychological pain of continuing the lion niche story. An occupier of this niche can only be warned that, in these days of the liberated lioness, his pride is likely to come before a fall.

"DON'T LET THAT 'MEMBER OF THE CAT FAMILY' INFLUENCE YOU. THE WORD IS 'ROAR', NOT 'MEOW'."

Chapter 11

The African Cobra Niche

The term cobra refers to a number of species of snakes classified in the genus *Naja*. They are found in Africa and Southeast Asia. The Asian species may attain a length of 18 feet. As a group they are extremely intelligent, aggressive, and venomous. Among the most notorious members of the genus are the spitting cobras of Africa. These creatures have the nasty habit of rearing up and shooting out a charge of venom toward the unfortunate victim. They aim with considerable accuracy for the eyes and can hit a target as far away as twelve feet. The venom causes considerable pain and temporary blindness, so that the target animal is totally distracted while the cobra goes about its business without fear of counterattack.

Ogden Nash, with his characteristic brevity, summed up many of the features of this strange reptile:

The cobra fills his mouth with venom
And walks upon his duodenum.
He who meets up with the cobra
Will soon be a sadder he
And sobra.

The organizational cobra, of necessity, occupies a position of functional importance. Certainly no one in an organization would tolerate the cobra's venomous attacks upon the ego if the victim were not utterly dependent upon the noxious beast for the performance of a necessary task. This kind of cobra has a propensity for attacking people at all levels in the hierarchy, so that no one is safe from the poison he ejects with faultless aim.

In truth, the occupant of the cobra ego niche is using an incredibly efficient psychological ploy. Everyone else in the organization is so busy staggering around blindly and writhing in pain from his attacks that no one notices all the faults, errors, and inadequacies in the cobra himself. As a result, his work goes unchecked and he can do pretty much as he pleases.

The cobra usually occupies a solitary office, or nest, somewhat camouflaged by the books, papers, bulletin boards, wall charts, and other paraphernalia appropriate to the organization's function. The *Naja* analog is never far from a telephone, and is as adept at interjecting his poisonous juices into the far-reaching wires as at directing it upon an immediate victim.

Probably you are all too familiar with the scenario we are about to relate, yet, painful though it may be, it is worth the retelling.

You have some documents to process, which require the expert attention of Ms. Naja. You are in a genuine hurry about this processing, and nothing will serve as a substitute for a direct meeting with herself. You stand outside her office door, hands sweating, heart palpitating, dreading the moment of truth. You knock on the door, and a voice from within snarls "Wait a minute!" You can hear that she is on the telephone and that someone at the other end of the line is getting the full treatment. Your nerve fails, you want to run away.

Suddenly an idea penetrates your quaking mind: today you will charm the snake. You will be so pleasant, so utterly beguiling and disarming, that she will not strike, she cannot possibly strike.

"Come in!" says the summons. You enter.

"Good morning, Ms. Naja. My!, you're looking very cheerful today," you lie through your teeth. "My goodness! Your office looks different!—Have you done something to fix it up?"

"What do you want?" she hisses.

Not yet blinded and broken, you continue your efforts. "I'm especially happy to see you today, because I have some business that requires your expert attention. I'm sure that no one else could handle so well a matter of such subtle difficulty."

She glowers. "I'm busy! Can't you tell me what you want?"

"I need these documents put in appropriate form for a bid on a state contract," you say, handing her a sheaf of papers.

"Why didn't I get these two weeks ago? Why the hell does everyone in this office expect me to bust a gut doing everything at the last minute? Besides, you haven't filled out Form 230 to go with these. You know I can't do a thing without Form 230. Furthermore, your worksheets were two days late last week. And your section has overspent its budget by sixty-three cents. You people out there are supposed to know your job. You've also used more pencils than anyone else, and someone from your group left some scrap paper on the Xerox machine. I don't run a garbage service, you know."

By now you are reeling with pain, blinded by the poison.

Even worse! Your ignoble mind, too, is cracked. Wide open. You have perceived, in the instant, the full meaning of the old Sanskrit proverb: "To feed a cobra with milk, without first taking out its poison fangs, is only to increase the flow of venom."

Such a cobra can cause considerable anguish in an organization in spite of its being efficient and productive. The reason is obvious: people who want to protect their own egos (and breathes there the one who does not?) are so determined to evade the cobra that they contrive all kinds of ruses to avoid dealing with that vicious individual. Such a variety of obscure pathways, hidden shunts, and distant end-runs are sought to avoid crossing the cobra's path! Such a vast amount of energy is wasted in escaping the wrath of the spitter! Simple procedures are made very complex, and the procedural ladder becomes an elaborate network, a veritable rat's run of crossing and interconnecting pathways. Jobs go unfinished because doing them involves facing the cobra. Thus, the *Naja* ego niche is protected at the expense of the organization.

One cobra I know has an office next to a viper, relatively inoffensive by comparison. One day Ms. Naja reared up her head, slitted her eyes in the direction of the next office, and sneered: "I knew her when she didn't have a pit to hiss in."

Chapter 12

The Sand Crab Niche

Walk along a seaside someday, and notice the small creatures scurrying about on the sand. See how each one skitters sideways into his hole, only to emerge a few minutes later to dump a load of sand and then hurry back into the temporary home he is digging. Observe the activities of these little crustaceans for a long period of time. Note how the wind and the waves are constantly moving sand around so that the crab's holes are being filled in, perpetually.

This is the fate of these poor ten-footed animals. Talk about poor Sisyphus! Crabs are forever running about, but are always moving sideways, so that they never go anywhere. And in sand they ceaselessly dig holes that are forever being filled up. But yet they survive.

Such is the career of the person who elects to fill the sand crab niche. He defends his position by giving the appearance of being constantly busy at his job. In this the sand crab niche resembles the beaver niche. But the organizational sand crab is basically incompetent. All his busyness succeeds only in moving him sideways, never forward. He is always digging holes that are always being filled in—by time, or tides, or fellow workers.

Witness a sad example of this creature at work. Joe Crustacean is a salesman who barely ekes out a living as a representative for a commercial hardware distributor. His day begins early, as he takes a list of potential customers and scuttles off to see them. He does not analyze the list to set himself some likely priorities, but simply jumps into his car and rushes off. He hurries from one customer to another, not bothering to learn the customer's needs or to pick up any other information that would help him in selling the line he represents. He sees more customers per day than most salesmen do in a week, but he rarely sells anything. He is going no-where, but he is going there fast.

One of the most pleasant, if least interesting, people in an organization in which I once worked was the very paradigm of a sand crab. He was so quiet, so unobtrusive, that I never knew his name or his job title, although he was an employee of the Buildings and Grounds Division. Each morning he would come into every office, turn on all the lights, and check which bulbs needed changing. Since the fluorescent bulbs almost never needed replacement on this time scale, he went to his next task, which was checking filters in the heating and air-conditioning ducts. Since filters almost never needed changing on this time scale, he proceeded to his next task which was a solitary and ritualistic coffee break. Then he skittered off to the subsequent job, which seemed to consist of moving boxes of toilet tissue and paper towels from one side of the storage room to another, with the ostensible purpose of locating something under the pile. That done (with what success I never learned), he went off to lunch and was rarely seen in the afternoon. Apparently he dug a hole in the sand somewhere, wherein he awaited the arrival of high tide—which always occurred at four-thirty, when he scurried out of the building.

One can hold only a neutral attitude toward the sand crab.

No true emotion is weak enough to describe the response that he evokes.

The sand crab ego niche is a common one for hapless students who write meaningless thirty-page papers full of verbiage and errors, instead of the three-page report that was wanted.

Perhaps the sand crab niche would not have been worth the effort of even this brief discourse had not T.S. Elliot given us such a deep, tragic, and poignant view of the human sand crab in J. Alfred Prufrock. The pitiable Prufrock perceived the crustacean character of his place in the world when plaintively, he said:

"I should have been a pair of ragged claws
Scuttling across the floors of silent seas."

In his final lament he returned to the theme:

"We have lingered in the chambers of the sea
By sea-girls wreathed with seaweed red and brown
Till human voices wake us, and we drown."

If you have a sand crab in your organization, the best thing to do is to slow him down, by brute force if necessary, and try to direct him into the tortoise track: there he will be slow, perhaps, but at least he'll be going straight ahead.

Chapter 13

The Giraffe Niche

One of the most unusual beasts of the African plains is the giraffe, the tallest of all mammals, which may soar more than eighteen feet from hoof to head. This lofty but small-headed creature towers over the rest of us and views the world from a haughty vantage point. To really understand the giraffe, we must understand how he got to be this way; that is, we must recognize the evolutionary pressures among his ancestors that led to a selection for long necks.

The giraffe is an herbivore that evolved in Africa in company with a number of other species of large herbivores. Those animals competed for grass, leaves, and other kinds of forage, which sometimes was in limited supply. Consider, then, the members of a species that developed mutations toward longer legs and longer necks. Such a species could reach leaves growing higher on trees, in branches and twigs, that were unavailable to other and squatter species. Thus a supply of foodstuffs was made available to the giraffes for which other herbivores could not compete. Such a mutation obviously would have an advantage over lower forms in times of food shortage. A series of such mutations would make available to the lengthening giraffe more and more food that no other animal could claim. Just looking at a giraffe tells us that such a sequence of mutational events must have occurred to present him with those splendidly extended legs and that

73

magnificently elongated neck. The giraffe enjoys a unique ecological niche: he's a member of the second trophic level eating high off the first trophic level, up to eighteen feet high.

The giraffe, because of its large size, is relatively free from predators. Moreover, because of its unique ecological niche, it is relatively free from competition for food. Thus the giraffe lives in a world of its own, with its head in the clouds so to speak, above the storms and stresses of the intensely savage competition among creatures in the world below. This unusual creature reacts to threats of danger by running away—an easy escape, because of its long legs. Scientists have blessed this animal with a mellifluous name: *Giraffa camelopardalis.*

Among human counterparts, as might be expected, the giraffe ego niche tends to appear in the upper levels of an organization's hierarchy if only because the giraffe's degree of aloofness is somewhat inconsistent with the functional necessities at the more productive lower levels. The human giraffe has his head in the clouds and avoids ego involvement with colleagues either by being serenely aloof from everything that happens about him, or by stretching his long legs and loping off to another high tree to nibble upon. Because of their aloofness, organizational giraffes often appear to be very profound or very concerned. Whereas the truth is, they really don't give a damn. They have found a niche that protects them from the savage realities of the institution's operations, and they exploit that niche to the fullest extent.

Consider the case of Mel Pardalis, Dean of Students at a college of medium size.

Secretary: "Sir, a delegation of students is here to see you. They're complaining about the food in the dining halls and the fact that ninety-three students were in the infirmary last week with food-poisoning, suspected of being caused by *Salmonella.*"

Dean : "You *know* I can't see them now. I'm busy preparing my talk on the Neo-Adlerian Psychology of Student Unrest. Send them to the Head of Dining Halls. That's his business. After they've gone, please go to the library for me and get copy of Heffelfinger's *Analysis of Glot's Critique of Dewey's Theory of the Educational Process.* Oh, and also *Medieval Southern Albanian Poetry*, by Czryjx."

Two days later, the Dean's secretary reappears like an unlaid ghost. "Sir, the students are here again. You know, complaining about the dining hall. They are very angry. I think you had better see them."

Dean: "Too bad. Just when I was beginning to perceive the relationship between student unrest and the oriental root of Camus' relation to Ezra Pound. Well, can't be helped, I guess. Send 'em in."

Students: "Sir, we just can't stand the garbage being dished up around here. It's poison, and the portions are so small."

Dean: "As you know, I have always been the chief advocate of the rights of students. I will act directly, you can be sure. But, ladies and gentlemen, please do not allow this passing affair of the gastrointestinal tract to interfere with the true cerebral activity of a liberal education, which is the reason why you and I are here. Rest assured. Your problem will be dealt with."

Two days later, Miss Loyal Secretary is back, wringing her hands, tearful behind her *pince nez*: "Sir, the students have seized the dining hall!!! They're threatening to tar and feather the dietician!"

Dean: "Darn! Always interruptions. And just when I was getting at the pure essence of the ontology and epistemology of student dissent.—Get my file on Vincent Lombardi and the Aztec Sacrifice Ethic. I must leave now. I've got to get away from this bedlam. I'm going to my house in the country to finish this manuscript. It's due in two days. Then I'll be away for a week at the Educational Association Meeting where I shall be leading a panel on Understanding Our Students. Oh, by the way, before you forget, notify the campus police about this fuss at the dining hall."

The giraffe can be found in many different kinds of organizations. In religious hierarchies, he is the bishop who is meditating upon the infinite potential of man, the while his parish is experiencing an unemployment rate of 34 percent. In business institutions, he is the economist who worries over the cyclic versus the linear theories of production, the while his company's creditors are demanding a reorganization of its management. In government departments, he is the savant who ponders whether the county or the city is the proper constitutional entity to be delegated as the authority for controlling the release of solid effluents into public waterways, while ignoring the prime fact that, already, the lake in question is dead.

An organization can tolerate the presence of a giraffe only when he is surrounded by loyal assistants who will meet his responsibilities, do his work, and occasionally stick out their necks for him.

Chapter 14

The Chicken Niche

One of the most important discoveries concerning animal behavior in recent years has been the phenomenon of dominance among domestic fowl. If a flock is observed, different birds are seen to peck at others, in a hierarchical arrangement that is called "the pecking order." By carefully following the identity of individuals, human observers have established the fact that all the members of an entire flock are so ordered that each will peck only those lower down on the social ladder. In addition, birds tend to peck only at others near them in social rank, and therefore only slightly lower in status. They ignore fowls that are far below them in the barnyard's scheme of things.

This ordering behavior, which was first noticed in the domestic chicken, *Gallus domesticus,* appears to be widespread among social animals. The niche is especially prevalent in those organizations that are rigidly hierarchical in nature, and resembles a food chain rather than a feeding network. It can best be presented by illustration.

Department Chairman Cox is addressing a meeting of full professors in a major department at Barnyard College: "Gentlemen, as you know, our introductory course has not been revised for forty-seven years, and there have been some recent complaints about its relevance, whatever that is. In addition, the textbook is now out of print. I am appointing an

Ad Hoc Committee, to consist of Professor G. Gallus as chairman, ably assisted by Professor Rock Cornish and Professor Dwight Leghorn, to offer suggestions as to how to undertake the course revision. *Ab ovo*, if I may be allowed to add a word of advice. . ."

Two weeks later the scholars report back to the senior faculty with the recommendation that a working committee be named to draw up a revised course outline. The Ad Hoc group further advises that the working section be composed of Associate Professor Reed Bantam, Associate Professor C. Fowler, and Associate Professor Minorca Black. The suggestion was endorsed unanimously. After two further weeks of effort, the working committee responds to the chairman.

Associate Professor Reed Bantam: "Professor Cox, we have formulated a skeleton outline to embody the philosophical changes in the course structure, but we feel that the detailed outline and implementation should better be left to the non-tenured faculty, who have much more contact with the introductory students and will be better able to judge the level of difficulty of the material. We suggest, as being especially appropriate to these needs, Assistant Professor Rose Wyandote, Assistant Professor Rock Plymouth, and Assistant Professor Al Ova."

The chairman, duly impressed by the wisdom of the advisory committee, appoints the implementation committee. After three weeks of gallunt labor they produced a four-page detailed outline and sat down with the chairman to discuss their work.

Assistant Professor Rose Wyandote: "We have now

produced a detailed outline of the course. Each of the major sections should be written up as a chapter for an introductory book. We recommend that we provide teaching experience for the graduate assistants by allowing them to each write one chapter of this work."

The wisdom of so generous a suggestion was applauded, and the graduate assistants were allowed to peck freely around in Barnyard's campus until the chapters were produced. The entire sequence finally resulted in a book, soon acclaimed as a classic *Introduction to the Nature of Democratic Societies*, by Cox, Gallus, Cornish and Leghorn.

The chicken niche, honored though it is in institutions of higher education, is nowhere more visable than in the military, where the entire vocabulary is replete with reference to domestic fowl, the excreta of domestic fowl, and numerous other barnyard subjects and activities. The following excerpt is taken (with permission) from an unofficial history of the United States Navy, as yet unpublished.

Admiral Jake Coprolite: "Captain Ordure, as I passed the parade ground this morning I noticed three gum wrappers, two cigarette butts, and one used tampon. Let's get this base ship-shape! Do you read me?"

Captain John Ordure got on the phone as soon as the Admiral left and called his second in command, Commander Frank X. Creta. "Frank, as I passed the parade ground this morning, I noticed three gum wrappers, two cigarette butts, and one used tampon (And a partridge in a pear tree, was the frivolous thought that passed through his head, only to be suppressed). Damn it man, this is a naval base, not a garbage dump. Get after it! Now!"

"TAKE IT EASY, BUDDY — I'M NOT IN YOUR PECKING ORDER."

Commander Creta, in a fit of rage, walked across the hall to the office of Lieutenant Commander "Chick" De Tritus and roared: "The old man passed the parade ground this morning and noticed three gum wrappers, two cigarette butts, and one used tampon. What the hell kind of executive officer are you, to have a base looking like that? Now move it!"

As soon as Creta left, De Tritus got on the intercom: "Now hear this! Company C get out there on the parade ground, now! Pick up every piece of trash—I said *every*. If I see a single piece of trash there by 0900, all leaves and liberties are cancelled for two weeks."

Later that day, as Lieutenant Commander De Tritus arrives at his home, he notices that the garage window is broken. Since it is his policy to run his house in a shipshape manner, he strides in, kisses his wife (once), and says: "Bosun, pipe the crew." She hauls out a bosun's whistle and blows a shrill call. Three lads, ages six, eight, and ten appear on the instant, and line up at attention before their parents. The Lieutenant Commander announces: "We are now meeting as a Court of Inquiry. Who broke that window?"

"Not I, Sir," says the ten year-old.

"Not I, Sir," says the eight year-old.

"I did," says the cool six year-old.

The senior officer paces back and forth. "We are now dismissed as a Court of Inquiry and are convened as a Court Martial." A five-minute trial ensues, terminating with the chief judge (the same Lt. Commander De Tritus no less) announcing: "Before I pass sentence, do you have anything to say in defense of yourself?"

The six year-old stands erect. "Yes sir. How do I get

transferred out of this chicken-shit outfit?"

So much for the chicken ego niche.

Chapter 15

The Frog Niche

It's almost impossible, while watching a frog or toad leaping about in an apparently random manner from one spot to another, not to be reminded of some organizational associate whose ego is guarded by leap-frogging from one subject or one place to another to avoid confronting any real problems. Nature's leaping amphibians lack tails and have long powerful hind legs with which to thrust themselves forward so that they are somewhere else before the predator has decided where they are. The true frog belongs to the genus *Rana,* but the entire order Salientia possesses the trait that is of immediate interest. The organizational frog may exist at almost any level and we will present the extremes to illustrate the point. At the first trophic level the jumping is almost entirely physical, while at the upper levels it is largely verbal.

The first example is a plumber, Burgess Oscar Canorus, known to his friends as Bufo. Bufo had been in the organization for a long time and was the odd jobs plumber for Buildings and Grounds. His modest abilities had reached their limit and he developed a healthy distaste for work. Survival being what it is, Bufo developed a strategy—the frog ego niche.

One day T.S., a junior executive, noticed an overflowing toilet in the junior exec's wash room. He responded in true heroic fashion by rushing back to his office and shouting at his secretary to call for assistance. The ever efficient Miss Typo called the appropriate number and asked for a hydraulic helper in a hurry.

The supervisor answered, "If you're in a big hurry, try to get Bufo, he's fixing a drain in the darkroom in building C."

A call to the photo processing laboratory brought the reply, "He left for the stockroom to get a part."

The next logical step, as if a frog could employ such Aristotelian abstractions as logic, was to try the stockroom. "Oh, Bufo got here at coffee break time, try the cafeteria."

The cafeteria announced that he had left for an emergency at central shipping, a busted pipe or something.

By this time the flooding water had inundated the orders department and an entire organizational search located him in his mechanics jumpsuit drinking at the water fountain. Doubtless a lily pad would have served as well.

A far more elaborate niche may be constructed by a frog high up in the hierarchy. The case of Ron Pipiens will bring the problem into focus. The ambitious Mr. Pipiens had worked himself up to be the head of his division, but once there his lack of imagination kept him from knowing what to do with his new found authority. He avoided even the hint of a decision by jumping ceaselessly from one thing to another.

Witness the following events when one of the section heads in Mr. Pipiens department, Ernest Fellow, came to see his supervisor.

Fellow: "Mr. Pipiens, there's an important and urgent problem I'd like to have you make a decision on. We're having a jurisdictional dispute between carpenters and sheet metal workers as to who should install the metal covered wood frame partitions."

Pipiens: "Oh yes, let me see now, do you remember the jurisdictional problem between machinists and custodians over metal filings?" Mr. Pipiens entered a long monologue about an event that had occurred before unionization many years previously. He was finally interrupted.

Fellow: "I've read both contracts and the language is vague enough to indicate we've a real problem."

Pipiens: "Oh yes, the contract language. I remember a contract we once had with Acme wire. It had some vague language and we ended up in the courts. Funny thing about court cases, the settlement is almost always out of court. It's a technique the lawyers have. Do you remember when Donaldson was company attorney? He really took us through some strange cases. Donaldson was an odd type though. He used to jog into work every morning."

Fellow: "I thought we ought to get the two shop stewards together and try to reach some kind of accomodation before they both walk out."

Pipiens: "Good idea, we don't want a wildcat strike on our hands. I remember the first year I was with this company; there was a wildcat strike at our competitors that kept them closed for three months. Gee, it's been nine years now since Monarch Corporation went out of business. That treasurer they had paid more attention to his golf game than his job. By the way, did you see the Arizona Open on TV last Sunday? Some really remarkable putting. The greens were super fast. They must have to water that grass all the time in Arizona. Which reminds me, we could use some rain. I don't think we've had a dry spell like this in over six years. Then we had that downpour that wiped out those bridges. They don't build enough margin of safety in small bridges. . . ."

An hour later Fellows excused himself and went to his office to try to figure out what to do about the jurisdictional dispute. Pipiens went off to three meetings he had to attend. He, somehow, had to be on so many committees that it really kept him hopping.

It is difficult to know what an organization can do about its frogs. One is reminded of Mark Twain's notorious jumping frog of Calaveras county. That animal was finally kept in one place by feeding him quail shot until he was too heavy to leap—which certainly recognizes the full gravity of the situation.

Chapter 16

The Human Niche

The last ego niche we shall consider is the most difficult of all to describe, because the peculiar species occupying this place exhibits such complex and irregular behavioral patterns. The natural niche and the ego niche can overlap completely in the species we refer to as *Homo sapiens,* man the wise. This designation of the genus, incidentally, is old in the history of western thought: as early as 1596 Shakespeare wrote, in *King Henry IV,* "Homo is a common name to all men."

In retrospect, it seems strange that the early taxonomists chose sapience, or wisdom, to identify a species which is characterized every bit as much by folly as it is by wisdom. It is interesting to speculate about how our view of ourselves might have been affected if the taxonomists of old had designated our species as *Homo stultus* or *Homo ineptus,* variations upon the theme of foolish man.

In view of our modern awareness of sexism and its attendant evils, it seems to have been no accident that the masculine designation was chosen as the generic name for the species. In doing so, the classifiers continued the old Graeco-Roman certainty that the word for "man" and for "person" are one and the same. A totally feminist society might have chosen *Femina sapiens* or *Mulier fecunda* as the scientific name of our species. Point of view is everything and prejudice is nothing more than pre-judgement.

If we who live in the world today hope to root out sexism, we must start from the beginning and rename our very species, in order to reflect our bisexuality in a more egalitarian manner. Therefore we propose that the name of our species be changed to *Hetero sapiens*, and we shall employ that unprejudiced designation for the remainder of this essay.

Perhaps our noble and open-minded example will start a conceptual revolution in this most important matter of identification, a subject that—at the present time, as in the past—has been so fertile a breeding ground for contention, misconception, and apprehension, if not more invidious evidence of warfare.

Understanding the place in society of the human ego niche requires going back into the evolutionary history of the species, in order to examine the behavioral characteristics that accompanied the transition of our ancestors from *Proconsul* to *Australopithecus* to *Homo erectus* to *Hetero sapiens*. Hundreds of millions of years ago, the primates, of which our species is a member, evolved from shrewlike animals which took to living in trees. Referring once again to Shakespeare, we see at last that the evolution of man can be regarded as the psycho-historical process of "the taming of the shrew." In view of our taxonomic closeness to the shrew, it seems a bit perverse that we hold such a bad view of this animal. Yet the Oxford Dictionary records some very unfavorable responses as the first three definitions of the noun shrew: "1) A wicked, evil-disposed, or malignant man; a mischievous or vexatious person; a rascal, villain; 2) A thing of evil nature or influence; something troublesome or vexatious; 3) A person, esp. (now only) a woman given to railing or scolding or other perverse or malignant behavior; freq. a scolding or turbulent wife."

Perhaps we ourselves are wise unto the moment for not undertaking to describe the shrew ego niche.

In any event, some of the early insectivores (or shrews) took to living in trees, and eventually evolved a grasping hand and binocular vision, with eyes placed at the front of the head, for depth of perception. In the course of many more millions of years this group became the Prosimians, or pre-monkeys. (The grasping hand of man seems to be such a highly developed characteristic of so many contemporary people that we can scarcely refrain from pursuing the fruitful research that would lead to a discourse on the Prosimian ego niche.)

Those early primates gave rise to the monkeys, the progenitors of the apes who presumably evolved when, with changing climatic conditions, vast areas of the African forest dried up and became grasslands and there was not enough room in the trees for the whole monkey population to dwell in. The monkeys who were pushed out of their arboreal habitat evolved in the direction of tail-lessness and an upright posture, which was certainly a more efficient way for them to get about in the open grasslands.

From one of these ancestral great apes evolved the line of descent of man. This relationship was understood more than 2000 years ago by keen observers. The Roman philosopher Quintus Ennius shook his head ruefully over the resemblance: "The ape, vilest of beasts, how like to us."

The early Hominidae (people-apes) had one big problem—getting enough food. In the jungle, fruits and nuts grow in plenty and are there for the taking. Before the days of farming, however, the grasslands did not yield very bountiful crops of grains, and what there was of them was quickly eaten up by the many grazing animals. The evolutionary solution for the people-apes was to move themselves up one trophic level, from the vegetarian mode of existence in the jungle to the carnivorous mode in the grasslands. The Hominidae began to eat the grazers.

But eating the grazing animals of the grasslands did not solve all the problems for our progenitors. The grazers were either so large and strong or so very fast that catching a meal on the run was a most difficult task. Thus the Hominidae learned to hunt in packs and to develop tools to help them kill the animals. This mode of obtaining food led to a selection for intelligence and cooperation. After all, the hunting pack was one of the first kinds of human organizations, and, in a sense, presages our emergence as *Hetero sapiens*. The social organization as a biological device is older than the species itself. Within this early hunting organization the penalty for failure was all too often swift and overwhelming. Failure to cooperate with members of the pack and to outwit the prey led to starvation or perhaps to being trampled beneath a stampeding herd of terrified beasts. Only by being clever and by working together were the ape people able to catch their prey.

During this hunting period territoriality developed as a strong factor for the species. Because of the extreme difficulty in catching food, it was imperative for each pack to be able to pursue its game without interference from other hunters. This was accomplished by marking a pack's territory to exclude intruders. Thus cooperation by members of the community within the bounds of the territory and antagonism toward members of other alien groups became part of the apparatus for survival of the emerging new species that one day would be man/woman.

"IF ONLY DARWIN COULD HAVE SEEN THIS."

With further evolution, gregariousness and rational processes, including methods of communicating thought, emerged as powerful survival mechanisms for the developing species. The concept of territoriality was extended to include the notion of a home, a place that each individual could call his own. Aggressiveness was not eliminated entirely, but was channeled into means of protecting the group's territory, and in defending its weaker members from enemy marauders. These altruistic concerns for others, rather than for the self, are some of the characteristics that distinguish humans from most animals.

Our brief discussion of the evolution of our species immediately suggests the description of an ego niche where a person uses intelligence, rationality, and cooperation to protect and defend his self-estimation. The very qualities which led to the emergence of modern *Hetero sapiens* are exploited to help the individual establish a satisfactory role. As a fascinating corollary, the closer an individual comes to possessing the ideal virtues described above, the less does his ego need defending. Such a person becomes an exception to our theory of ego niches and is able to carry out his or her organizational function to the full—and to the admiration of a few kindred spirits who can appreciate such rare excellence. Most of us, alas, fall short of this degree of near perfection. But all of us know a few heroes and heroines who have come close to achieving it.

The human ego niche starts with the idea of territoriality, a place within the organization, a job which a person understands and does well. The occupier of this niche carries out his responsibilities and takes quiet pride in defending the quality of his work. He may be somewhat aggressive, withal, but he channels that aggressiveness into tasks which aid his organization in performing its functions, without doing harm to the lives and egos of others.

The occupier of the human ego niche cooperates with his associates. His cooperativeness does not descend to mere make-work busyness, and he avoids the monkey business of our simian ancestors. He is intelligent, meaning that in his wisdom, he tries to seek rational solutions to problems, rather than relying on instinctive reactions, in the manner of the rest of the animal world. He is gregarious and feels genuine concern for his fellow workers. He tries to understand their ego hang-ups, and the ego defenses they have adopted. In doing so, he tries to help them attain the *Hetero sapiens* ego niche.

While this description of the ideal colleague may seem like a dream, let us remember that dreaming is also very much a part of our humanity. And, as the very young are already wise enough to know, how can you succeed, if you don't try?

Chapter 17

Et Cetera

Such examples of the infinite adaptability of the human animal can be extended far beyond the bounds of this exploratory report. Sadly, we shall leave unwritten our descriptions of the coral niche, the leech niche, the turtle niche, and the bitch niche. Such an obvious example as the laughing hyaena ego niche hardly needs much comment. The observant reader will doubtlessly think of a whole zoo full of creatures out of his own organizational experience. Propriety insists that we neglect niches formed by members of the phylum Platyhelminthes, the flatworms, those insatiable organisms characterized by a single opening to the alimentary canal, so that mouth and anus are the same orifice. Occasionally, however, one is compelled to remind one's foul-mouthed associates of this particular bit of biological lore. Even more exotic and perverse modes of biological behavior exist, and almost invariably each of these suggests an organizational counterpart among people. Even the cryptobiotic forms, which in a hostile environment may remain totally inert, practically in a state of suspended animation for twenty years or more, may come to life—to the surprise, if not the dismay, of all their colleagues.

Nature is incredibly rich and prolific in its forms. And her creatures have developed a prodigious number of survival strategies during the evolutionary history of the planet Earth.

Human beings too, are remarkable inventive and marvelously adaptable. They have to be in order to survive the traumata that assault them, constantly, both in body and in psyche. People within organizations have exploited an astonishingly wide range of tactics in the all-important effort to protect their egos. Devices hardly studied as yet by serious ethologists have been extensively if subconsciously employed since the dawn of civilization. Junior faculty members imprinted on senior colleagues long before Konrad Lorenz's classical work on geese appeared. Territoriality, within an organization, has been known for at least six millenia before Tinbergen began watching sea gulls pecking at each other. The oldest known example discovered so far goes back to the First Egyptian Dynasty, to the officer's club at Memphis established by Pharaoh Narmer in 4113 B.C.

From all this, at least one message is clear: ethologists should examine organizations, and specialists in industrial administration should study the work of ecologists and animal behaviorists. Pyramidal hierarchies, whether among men or among animals, will exhibit common features wherever they are found. We must posit a new science of pyramidal hierarchology. Founding a new science is an awesome thing, but the laws of nature push us inexorably onward, impelling us to call the attention of humankind to this inescapable pattern of organization. Perhaps because it is so omnipresent, so ingrained in the practices of men, it has escaped the attention of serious scholars.

As far as the practical consequences of our studies are concerned, only a brief summary is needed. First and foremost is the paramount fact: individuals in organizations do not check their egos at the door between the hours of nine to five.

Their egos accompany them as constantly as do their shadows. Indeed, we can best conceive of the situation with a paraphrase of Robert Louis Stevenson's famous poem presented here (with apologies to the poet's shade for this rendering):

My Ego

I have a little ego that goes in and out with me,
And what can be the use of it is more than I can see.
He is very like me, from the psyche within the head,
And fear of hurting him scares me when I jump into my dread.

He hasn't any notion of how adults ought to play,
And tries to make a fool of me in every sort of way.
He stays so close beside me, he's a coward you can see
I think it shameful to stick to people as my ego clings to me.

From the quintessential fact, we draw our one and only irrefutable rule. *Organizations must learn to live with egos, as egos have learned to live with organizations.*

The main purpose of this study has been the exposition of the bifunctional role of individuals within organizations. Two attitudes can emerge from such an investigation. Those people who are interested only in efficiency will lament the inevitable ego-generated snafus that will impede progress within the establishment. Those people who fear the total subjection of the individual in the machinery of the organization will hail our discovery of ego niches as proof that clever human beings have already found a way to save and salve their personalities in this world of digital dichotomy.